Becoming an eBay Power Seller

Tips and Tricks to Increase Your eBay Sales and Make More Money

By

Jay Johns

Disclaimer

This book is intended for educational purposes only and in no way guarantees any degree of success in online business. The author has made every attempt to verify that all information contained herein is correct to the best of his knowledge at the time of publication. However, this information is intended to be used as a reference by the reader. The author is in no way responsible or liable for any outcome that may result from a reader of this book entering into any form of online business activity. When selling on eBay as with any form of business you are entirely responsible for your level of success and for any outcomes, financial or otherwise, that result from your actions. Outcomes achieved vary from person to person based on level of skill, effort, and other circumstances. This book is purely a guide and does not guarantee any outcome; specifically, it does not guarantee any level of financial gain.

Also by Jay Johns

eBay Made Easy: How to Quickly and Easily Make Thousands of Dollars Selling Everyday Items Online

CONTENTS

Chapter 1 – Bigger and Better

So you've started selling on eBay and have discovered how regular, everyday people like yourself can make a pretty nice chunk of change just by selling random items. Things that you never in a million years thought there would be a market for, yet somewhere, someone wants them – and is willing to pay you for them.

It's magical, isn't it? When you first start selling on eBay you fall in love with getting that notification on your phone or in your email that you sold something and just like that, you have cash waiting for you! And just like so many other things, once you get a taste and realize not only how awesome it is but also how un-complicated the whole process can be, you want to figure out how to do more, more, more!

When you make your first bit of money on eBay you get bit by the bug and want to keep selling more and more. That's great, because it builds your entrepreneurial mindset and motivates you to keep going. There's definitely a leveling off point though, as just selling whatever you can come up with will only take you so far until you can't do any more in the amount of time you have.

If you're reading this book though it's likely that you've already experienced that feeling and are hungry for more. I'm going to assume you're not just dabbling in eBay to kill time, so you're looking for the knowledge and information you need to start making even more money while spending less time on eBay. It's absolutely critical to have a strategy that can grow your sales and to follow a systematic plan to continue moving upward. Too often people get bogged down in small details or tactics but don't have an overarching plan, so instead of making more money month over month and year over year they just stay at the same level and only end up spending more of their precious time.

The focus on **strategy** is what makes this book different from all of the other eBay selling guides and resources out there. It teaches you how to build a long term plan to grow your sales and create systems that will help you continue your growth.

This book is designed to be a quick and informative read so that you can get right to work instead of pouring over pages and pages of information that will take a long time to process. It is divided into four chapters, each one a key component of a well-rounded growth strategy.

The Importance of Strategy – This book will focus on four key elements that when used together can take you from making a little bit of money here and there to seeing consistent and increasing profits. The reason so many people fail to get beyond just mediocre results on eBay is because they focus only on tactics, or short term small things, instead of seeing the bigger picture and having a strategy.

The elements to successful growth are:

Finding your Niche

Pricing to Profit

Gaining Efficiencies

Repeating the Cycle

Combining these four elements will take you from a casual seller who makes a few dollars here and there from random sales to someone who has a healthy stream of profit coming in on a regular basis and satisfied customers who are returning to buy again and again.

Getting Started – Just Do It!

Once you have a clear plan, or at least a solid outline of one that incorporates all of these tenants, it's time to jump right in. That's it, just start doing exactly what this book says, no different than what you did after reading the first part. Don't worry about understanding every single detail; 75% of something more will always be better than doing nothing. Far too many people fall victim to "paralysis by analysis" or telling themselves that if they gather more information they're going to discover some magical insight that will all of a sudden make them successful.

The truth is that there is no magic formula. The way to sell more on eBay is to just learn more then roll up your sleeves and get to work. Even the strategies in this book, as good as they are and as valuable as they've been to so many people, aren't magic just by themselves. Reading something, absorbing it, and then going and doing it is the formula that will put you on the road to success.

So enough talk, it's time to get started on the road to becoming an eBay Power Seller!

Chapter 2 – Finding Your Niche

You likely got your start on eBay selling random items from your home that you don't need anymore. That approach is good because it brings in money and gets you excited about the idea of your 'junk' being worth cash. Getting paid builds your motivation to keep selling more. After a while though we all run out of random things to sell and are left scratching our heads trying to figure out what to do next.

Breaking Through the "Random Junk" Plateau – In my first few months on eBay my sales went up, up, up as I was learning the ropes and cleaning out my closets. Eventually though they hit a plateau while my home got neater and more organized. The way to get over this hump and start to take your eBay selling to the next level is to find a specific niche or category of items to sell.

There are certain things that I buy on eBay that I go right back to the same seller for every time. Why? Because I've bought from them before, they gave me what I wanted at a fair price, and I trust them. For them this is a success, because they now have a 'happy customer' instead of just a buyer. You can make random sales here and there and still make money, but this method will only take you so far. If you want to have a continuous stream of sales and the increasing profits that go with it you need a customer base of people who remember you and will buy from you again and again.

So how do you decide what your niche will be? It's not as complicated as you think. There are a few simple checks to ensure that you've picked one that's viable.

Interest: What Gets You Started Will Keep You Going – It's simple, yes—but having a strong interest in what you're selling is the first requirement for finding your niche. You have to get enjoyment from dealing with whatever it is that you're going to sell if you plan on sustaining it for the long term. If you're trying to sell something just because there's a lot of money in it you might be successful for a while, but eventually your lack of interest will take over and you'll slow down or stop altogether. For example, there can be a lot of money in electronics or antique coins on eBay but for someone who doesn't have an interest in either they wouldn't be good niches to get into.

Forcing yourself into any type of work, eBay included, just for the money inevitably becomes a daily drag. Tons of eBay sellers only make it a few months before they decided it isn't enjoyable enough to keep doing. Think the money could overcome that? It can, for a while—but eventually no amount of money will make up for lack of interest. We've all heard stories of people making six figure salaries climbing the corporate ladder that walk away and take jobs that pay considerably less but make them happier. Lesson learned: you have to enjoy what you're doing, so pick something to sell that you like working with first and foremost.

The Secret Weapon to Make You Stand Out From Other Sellers – Let's picture a guy named Jim, who sells mainly men's polo style golf shirts and button down dress shirts. Jim picked this niche because he literally wears one or the other every single day. He knows about different materials, cuts, brands, you name it. He knows what brands and styles other guys like him are wearing regularly. When buyers have questions he can answer them intelligently and give them a level of detail and information that makes them confident that he knows what he's talking about, because he does. It's not a chore to do his research on the items because his daily life is his research.

What's happening is that Jim is really just taking his own knowledge and using it to help him sell to others. He knows which kinds of shirts are lightweight and will ship for less, he knows which kinds will be in high demand in different seasons, he knows which kinds may seem like a good item to sell because they're from a certain brand but are actually in low demand because other guys like him don't really want them. This all translates into buyers seeing Jim as a cut above others who are selling the same things, so they're more likely to come back to him the next time they need a shirt.

Profit Margin and Demand: Can't Have One and Not the Other – Having a niche that will regularly bring good profits is key to getting to the next level of eBay. You can make a 'one off' sale of almost anything just on a fluke, but to keep the money coming in on a regular basis you need to be selling things that are proven profit makers. Having interest and knowledge alone aren't enough if your niche isn't one that buyers are regularly willing to pay a good amount of money for.

Getting even more specific with Jim's men's shirt example, let's say he sells Nike and Polo Ralph Lauren men's shirts because they consistently bring in good profits. These two brands are in demand because they're on the higher end of the men's clothing ladder, so the profits are healthier than with lesser-known brands. Jim knows this not only because he's done his pricing research that we'll discuss later on, but also because he's closely in tune to his target market and knows what brands and styles guys like him are wearing.

To illustrate the importance of having both a high margin and high demand, let's think about how Jim would do if he chose to sell a brand of shirts that everyone wanted but wasn't willing to pay more than a few dollars for. He'd be spinning his wheels listing, packing and shipping a ton of items and making very little money for it – definitely not the way to boost his profits.

In the opposite case, if Jim sold shirts that fetched huge profits but that not many people were interested in he'd make a nice haul every now and then but wouldn't have the regular sales to bring him continuous high profits. Finding an item that sits right in the middle of profit and demand is critical to choosing a sustainable niche.

Supply: Access and Renewal – The final piece of the puzzle is picking something that you have consistent access to and can keep getting more of to sell. Everything we've done so far, picking something we like, know about, and that will sell for good prices, won't do us much good if we can't keep getting our hands on more of these things to continue selling. To finish off Jim's men's shirts example, let's say there are about half a dozen thrift stores within 30 minutes of his home that he visits regularly and always finds Nike and Ralph Lauren men's shirts at. He goes to one or two each day and never fails to walk out with multiple shirts each visit. As Jim sells more he just restocks his inventory and his profits keep coming.

Finding something that you have a consistent supply of is critical to keep the machine going. This is where you have to again do your research or think creatively. Are you allowed to keep leftover supplies, parts, or other things that usually get thrown away at your job but will sell on eBay? Do you live in an area where certain items are readily available, such as near a famous attraction that people are looking for merchandise from as collectables? Think about what you have access to (legally of course) that you're interested in and has shown that it sells well; these items will be your sources of consistent profit.

We'll dive deeper into how you use this to build a base of satisfied, repeat customers later down the road. For now, your assignment is to go through the steps we've covered and identify a few viable candidates of items you can sell. Think of things that meet all the criteria: you enjoy dealing with them, you know a lot about them, they sell for good profits, and you have a consistent supply of them. When you identify things that fit this profile you're well on your way to accelerating your eBay sales!

Chapter 3 – The Price is Right

This chapter is very short, but critical to understand if you want to increase your sales and make more money on eBay in less time. One of the most common mistakes both beginners and even more experienced sellers make on eBay is setting prices too low, thinking they'll attract more customers. People get eager to make sales and fall victim to the trap of thinking "If I'm the lowest price I'll sell faster than the rest" or "If I just lower the price that'll bring in more sales and I'll make up for it in volume."

Both are wrong and can cost you a lot of money over time.

When you first start out it's true that any sale is a good sale. After a while though you have to get past the initial thrill of the sale and price your items so they can deliver a consistent stream of revenue for you. That means getting past the initial 'thrill of the sale' and making sure that the money you bring in is worth the time you spend on eBay.

If you have the lowest prices you'll end up fooling yourself into thinking that you're making money, because once you subtract out the eBay fees, PayPal fees and shipping costs for your item you can end up shocked to find out that you're working for near minimum wage if not less. It's probably not a stretch to say that you're not using your precious free time to get a return of only a few bucks an hour, right?

So how do you know where to price your item so it will make you money that's worth your time?

Doing Your Research to Find the Sweet Spot – Using this, you can validate that your niche is a profitable one (if you find that your items aren't selling for much you should go back through the steps in Chapter 1 and find a new niche) and also pick the 'sweet spot' where you need to price your items. There's no need to use any complicated math, just see what the majority of similar items are selling for and price yours the same. There are always going to be outliers that sold for way less (people who priced at the bare minimum just to make a sale) and way more (people who set a high price and got lucky) but you'll quickly see the price range where the majority of sales fall which is where you need to set your price.

Do some research on your items and you'll probably find that you're leaving money on the table with your prices. While setting a price unreasonably high will obviously turn buyers away, pricing low in hopes of undercutting everyone else doesn't necessarily lead to more sales. I experimented with this for a month once, setting my prices way lower to see if the adage about 'making it up in volume' was really true. It wasn't. I actually sold about the same number of items that I did at my regular prices, so trying to price low only led to me giving away money. Every item has its own 'sweet spot' where you can make a healthy profit and still sell consistently. Your assignment from this chapter is to find that spot by researching the prices that your item regularly sells for and to price yours accordingly.

Chapter 4 – Gain Efficiencies

Now that you've identified your specific niche, validated that it's profitable, and priced your listings so you can make consistent sales, you're ready to really kick things into gear. As we all know far too well, there are only so many hours in the day and we all have obligations and responsibilities we have to tend to.

Finding time to sell on eBay is difficult enough, so if you're not doing it in the most efficient way possible you're reducing your opportunity to profit as much as you can for your time. When you're randomly selling anything under the sun you have to spend more time researching and preparing each listing, so the return on your time is less than when you have a system in place that allows you to only spend a few minutes per item.

The following steps will make you more efficient throughout all phases of the eBay sales process, from listing to shipping to the rest of the administrative tasks like leaving feedback and answering buyer questions.

Go Mobile – Today we use our smartphones and tablets for so much—did you know they can also make your eBay selling easier and better as well? The eBay mobile app can save you a ton of time and allows you to be incredibly responsive to buyers. Anyone who is serious about their eBay selling should get it and start using it immediately! The best part is that it's free so you can download it today and be up and running in minutes.

Remember when we talked about how to know what an item will sell for? Well here's where the app is a huge help—you can do this same research with it, so whenever you're out looking at items you just pull out your phone to find out if something has resale value and is worth picking up. This works great when you're at thrift stores or garage sales and you see something that you think might sell but aren't sure about. Here's an example of how simple it is to do a quick price check on the mobile app. You can apply all of the same filters to your price search using the app that you can from your computer, so there's never a reason to be in the dark about whether an item is profitable.

You can also answer buyer questions on the fly with the app so you'll lose fewer sales opportunities to time. If someone is interested enough that they message you with a question they're serious enough about buying, so keep them warm by getting back to them with a quick response. You can be away from your computer anywhere and still make buyers feel like you're right there as their own in-store salesperson ready to answer their questions. I make note of this in my listings, letting buyers know that I'm super responsive and if they message me with a question I'll respond promptly.

Feedback is another area that you can handle quickly and easily via eBay mobile. Just go to one of your sold items and find the 'Leave Feedback' button and then enter your comments and you're done. You can take care of 'administrative work' like this when you have some short down time like waiting at an appointment or even in line at the grocery store or on the treadmill so you don't have to worry about it when you're busy actually working on your main eBay tasks like listing and shipping.

The app also lets you manage the Best Offer process if you use it on your listings so again you're being incredibly responsive to buyers who are ready to buy from you. Just like messages, all you have to do is click the 'Respond' button and you can either accept an offer or make a counter offer and include a note about conditions or anything else you need to let the buyer know.

Finally, you can create and edit listings and upload photos right from the app. I mention this last though because I don't actually recommend creating most of your listings this way. There are much more quick and efficient ways to do it that we'll cover later in this book, but this feature of the app is very helpful if you're away from your computer for a long time and need to get something listed. It also helps if you're doing a random proofread of your listings (I highly recommend you do this regularly) and notice a mistake that you need to fix.

Just like the other features in the app everything is very simple, just follow the prompts and you're all set.

Having the ability to promptly address buyers will put you a cut above the vast majority of eBay sellers, so get and use the eBay mobile app. It will make you able to be responsive to buyers which will always lead to more sales instead of letting them slip away due to time passed.

Stop Wasting Your Time! – Creating item listings is the biggest source of time drain for eBay sellers. Between taking photos, uploading them, writing descriptions and setting shipping information many sellers get frustrated at the amount of time they spend just to get a few items up for sale and give up on eBay because the money isn't worth the time. If you continue working in this fashion that'd be a pretty accurate statement, the money you'll make likely won't be worth the hours you put in. By mastering some simple strategies though you can develop an efficient and repeatable way of listing common items fast that you're trading your time for dollars instead of cents.

Process and automation are the keys to efficient listing. Having a set and defined way of doing things so you can go back to it again and again is how you get faster and accomplish more in the same time. When I first started selling on eBay I'd do a lot of listing on Sunday afternoons while watching football. I would list each item from start to finish one by one, taking photos, then typing out the description, selecting the item specifics and setting the price and shipping, then repeating for my next item. At the time it was great because I was getting ten or so items done in a single session. This was good as a beginner, but when I started to grow more and more I realized that this was nowhere near the best way to list.

Doing listing tasks in batches is by far better. Gathering up a set of items that are ready for sale and taking all the photographing at once, followed by all of the actual listing, and even pre-packing the items so that when they sell all you have to do is print the shipping label will save you tons of time. Here are the ways to make this happen:

The Assembly Line Photography Method – I shudder at the hours I wasted early on when I'd photograph items one by one. Today my garage becomes a true assembly line when I'm listing. I hang white shower curtains on all four walls and go around the room photographing dozens of items in just a few minutes quickly and effectively. When I'm done I pop the memory card out of my camera and drop the entire batch of photos onto my computer so I can go right to making my listings. Another way to do this is to upload the photos directly to an online storage site like Dropbox or Google Drive if you take pictures using your smartphone camera. The cameras on today's phones produce very high quality photos and will work perfectly for eBay. Once the pictures are transferred then you can get online and start putting up your listings for the same batch of items, no going back and forth from photo shoot to computer and wasting time.

Create it Once, List it Thousands of Times – We talked earlier about the importance of finding a niche because it allows you to become an expert on a particular item and streamline your operation. Here is where you will really see the results of that. Having a niche makes your eBay work much easier because it's repeatable. When you're using the 'sell random stuff' approach every single listing you put up is different from the last and the next which means you'll have to create it from scratch, clicking every dropdown menu and writing a unique description for everything you sell. This is incredibly time consuming and directly causes the 'leveling off' that usually hits so many eBayers. We all only have 24 hours in a day and at some point you just won't be able to (or want to) spend any more on eBay.

When you're selling the same items over and over again just with different variations such as color, size, model or brand you can start to work efficiencies like bulk listing and pre-made templates into your plan. Some sellers can get pretty complicated with their approach, but it doesn't have to be that way if you just follow the basics. Let's go back to our buddy Jim, and using his men's shirt example, look at how to take a listing that's already active and turn it into another one in just a few seconds. eBay has a 'Sell Similar' function that lets you copy a listing so you have all of the details set from your first item and just change out the ones that you need to. In this case Jim takes his listing for a men's Nike Golf polo shirt, color Red and Size XXL, and clicks 'Sell Similar' to start with a pre-filled listing for the exact same thing. If he has another of the same shirt in orange and size Medium he just makes those changes in the title and from the dropdowns and is all set, the rest of the details like style, size type and the price and shipping information stay the same.

When it comes to the Item Description if you're dealing with a similar item you can just edit a few words and be done instead of re-writing the entire thing. There are even some more advanced tricks like using spreadsheet programs to populate the same paragraph body with the different item details from a list, but for starters just getting to this point is going to save you a tremendous amount of time. Knowing what I do now I can't even imagine the days when I made every listing from scratch. That's the power of finding your niche, you move from just haphazardly putting stuff up for sale to having an actual system that can work for you and list double, triple, or even more items in the same time.

Once you really get rolling, you can take listing efficiency a step further by using an automated software program. TurboLister is a program made by eBay and available for free that allows you to import thousands of listings at a single time by filling out a spreadsheet with the necessary information and uploading it to eBay. This requires a bit of computer knowledge beyond just basics, but isn't difficult to learn by any means.

There are other similar software programs provided by third party companies outside of eBay that will interface with eBay to list items in bulk with various other features. Some of the more common ones are Auctiva and Inkfrog. Most of these programs are paid subscription programs though, so when you're first starting out with automated listing Turbo Lister is your best bet to learn the skill and get your own process down for free. We'll talk all about stuff like that further down the road, but for now I'd leave it alone and just make a mental note of it for later on.

Print Shipping Labels in Bulk – As a new eBayer you probably weren't selling more than a single item at a time so bulk packing and shipping likely never crossed your mind. When you get more items listed and some momentum in sales it will become normal to have days where you sell several items. Being efficient with your packing and shipping methods becomes more critical at this point. eBay offers the capability to print dozens of shipping labels at a time in one file so you don't have to individually print and repeat for each item but instead can print out all of the labels for your sold items that are currently paid for along with a mailing list to tell you which one goes with which package.

In this chapter, we talked about how to escape the perils of lost time that result from doing things the casual seller's way

– inefficiently. To drive increased sales you need to be able to list more items in the same or less time. In turn you also have to support more listings by answering buyer questions and packing and shipping sold items in a more efficient manner too. Using these key strategies will help you get far more done so that you can continue growing. The great thing about the advice in this chapter is that you can start implementing all of it right away, so your assignment is to do none other than start using the information you just read here!

Chapter 5 – The Most Overlooked Sales Booster

Feedback is one of the biggest areas that new or even intermediate eBayers overlook since it's natural to focus only on the here-and-now of trying to sell more without thinking of how you put yourself in a position to sell more in the first place. The typical eBayer looks at feedback as something that's 'nice to have' but doesn't understand the direct link between a higher feedback score and more sales. They also don't give much thought to what a high feedback score can do for their eBay operation over the long haul, again because they're narrowly focused on making the next sale but aren't mapping out a long term plan.

Your feedback score does two things—the first, which is what 99% of people think of, is that it shows your 'customer satisfaction rating' to any potential buyers. When you buy anything online you look at the reviews and see what percentage of people were pleased with the seller, and eBay is no different. People look at both the number of your score as well as the percentage of positive ratings you have, and some will even read the comments from others who have bought from you. That's pretty important, but it's only half of the story on how feedback helps or hurts your sales. Most eBayers don't know that there's an entire system of rankings and scoring going on behind the scenes and that your feedback score weighs heavily on the results of this system.

Understanding this is where you can truly leverage your feedback score to make you money. eBay's search algorithm uses a seller's feedback score as one of the factors in determining where to rank their item. Simply put, if you and I are both selling the same item and I have a higher feedback score than you do, all other things being equal my item will come up higher in the search results and buyers will see it before yours. Think of all of the would-be buyers who will already have found what they need at the and won't even lay eyes on your item if you have a low or even moderate feedback score because it's buried on the tenth page of search results.

Beginner eBayers approach feedback from a passive point of view and hope that their items and service are enough to make someone want to leave a high mark rather than actively working to keep their score going up and up. Getting to the next level takes a bit of work but, like most of the other things we've already talked about, also takes the right knowledge too so you're not just grinding away for little return.

Want to know the absolute best way that I've found to get buyers to leave positive feedback? It's actually pretty simple: ask them to do it.

Yep, that's it. Just ask for it. It's so simple, yet something that so many eBay sellers don't do. You'll be surprised how your positive feedback increases when you start actively asking buyers to leave it instead of just hoping that people will be nice enough to do it on their own. This isn't incredibly difficult either; it's something you can start doing in just a few minutes and make a regular system of so it doesn't take up a ton of your time.

In your list of sold items you'll see several little icons next to each item. One indicates whether the buyer has left feedback for the transaction or not. Each week, set aside time to go through your sold listings and send a message to each buyer who hasn't left feedback asking them to do it. It's simple and easy, just a quick note saying something like "Hi There- If you were satisfied with this item please leave 5-star feedback as I'll do the same for you as a buyer! Thank you!"

There are a few important things here: make sure you specifically ask for 5-star feedback. Directly telling the buyer what to do so they have less of a chance of getting confused or doing it haphazardly is key. eBay calculates your Detailed Seller Rating based off of the 1-5 'star' scores that your buyers leave you, so specifically calling out the term '5-star' will help guide people directly to giving you the highest mark. Also, let them know that you'll return the favor for them as a buyer. Some sellers will leave feedback as soon as a buyer pays for an item, but I don't recommend this because the transaction isn't truly complete yet. If a buyer gets the item and turns out to be unhappy and opens a case against you, the positive feedback that you left right away when they paid is still there. It's best to let the buyer leave feedback first to ensure that all is truly well with the sale and the transaction complete.

Even once you're actively asking buyers to leave feedback and are seeing your numbers increase, getting to a score of several hundred or thousand can still seem like it will take forever. Fortunately there's another easy way to speed it along. Your opportunity to receive feedback is directly proportional to how many sales you make, so you can open yourself up to receiving more feedback simply by making more sales. Every transaction counts the same in the feedback game regardless of whether it's a two dollar item or a two hundred dollar sale.

This simple tip, combined with the active asking we just discussed, worked great for me when I was just starting out on eBay and my feedback score was still in the double digits. Find some small and lightweight items that are easy to pack and you can get your hands on a lot of. Trinkets such as key chains or mini flashlights from a dollar store or deals at garage sales or flea markets where the sellers are offering an entire bag of things for only a few bucks work great. List all of the items (to make this tip work effectively and not become a time drain it's best that the items you use are the same or very similar, so you can create just one listing and keep selling them over and over again from it) and set the price low so you'd just break even after fees and shipping.

The key here is realizing that you're not selling these items to try and make a profit directly from them, but to set yourself up for future profits. Your goal is just to have a low priced item that will sell quickly and give lots of people the chance to leave you positive feedback (which you'll of course directly ask them to do a few days after the sale.) This is another example of how thinking strategically and working on a long-term plan can accelerate you beyond being just a casual seller.

Chapter 6 – Marketing to Get Repeat Customers

This is where you really separate yourself from all of the casual eBay sellers. Having a 'repeat' cycle in your strategy ensures that you're not just making more sales now, but that you're setting yourself up for continued growth and profit. To do this you need to build your reputation on eBay so that you're seen as a go-to source for the items that you sell, which is the first step toward winning repeat customers. A sale is a one-time event, but gaining a customer means you have someone who will return to buy from you again. If you earn a customer and keep them satisfied you'll make far more profit from this person than if you were to continue just making one off sales to anyone that happened to come across your listings.

It's no secret that more people seeing your stuff means more people who can buy your stuff, so your goal is to get as many people as possible to put their eyes on your listings. The core of selling anything is getting people to notice you and then forming a lasting impression in their minds. eBay is no different; once you do the hard work of getting your listings ranking high in searches and making sales you still need to turn your buyers into customers by getting them to come back and buy again, otherwise you're stuck just making one off sales like nearly everyone else.

The Easy yet Often Overlooked Marketing Tool – There's an extremely effectively marketing tool that far too many eBay sellers sabotage their success by overlooking in this digital age. It's proven to gain repeat customers and even referrals to other buyers, yet the majority of eBay sellers aren't taking advantage of it. It's a good old fashioned sales flyer. That's right, an actual piece of paper that has information from you straight to your buyer's hands. Think about it, when is the most opportune time to make an impression on someone and get them to remember you? How about the moment they open your package and hold the item that they've anxiously been waiting to receive.

Your 'sales flyer' can actually be something as simple as a small slip of paper that you print on your home printer. In fact, far too many sellers who lose sight of the forest among the trees by trying to cram as many logos and fancy designs as they can on to a business card so that it basically screams "I'm too confusing to read, just throw me away!" to the buyer when they open the package.

People buy from people they trust, so if you want to gain a repeat customer, building this trust is your first goal for your sales flyer. Reminding the buyer that if for any reason they're not satisfied with their experience you'll make it right lets them know that you want them to be satisfied and aren't just trying to make a buck off of them. People are quick to open up a case with eBay if they're not happy and feel like they didn't get the item or service they paid for. Seeing that you're honest and want to work to make them a satisfied customer will leave them far more willing to resolve any problems between the two of you instead of running to eBay right away.

The next goal of your sales flyer is to get the buyer to leave positive feedback for their experience. You can use the exact same technique of directly asking that we discussed earlier. The same message you send through eBay works great printed on your flyer; just a simple sentence asking the buyer to leave you 5 stars and letting them know you'll return the favor is all you need.

After you've got the buyer to leave positive feedback for this experience you now need to get them to return for another one. You can do this a number of ways, all of them centered on keeping your name fresh and memorable in the buyer's mind. A statement that has your seller name and tells the buyer *"Check Out my Other Items for More Great Deals!"* is extremely effective.

Here's a great word-for-word example of a sales flyer you can use. Just print these ten or twelve to a page and start including one in every package you ship:

If you're satisfied with this item please leave "5 STAR" feedback as I'll do the same for you! If you have any issues with your item contact me and I'll resolve them—I'm not happy until you're happy!

Check Out My Other Items for More Great Deals: Jims_Awesome_Shirts

If you're not including a small sales flyer in every package you ship out you should start yesterday! Follow this simple formula and you'll see your repeat customers, and sales, almost certainly go up:

Give the buyer a great experience + Make them feel like you're there for them + Let them know you'll do something good for them = They come back and buy again!

Making money on eBay isn't rocket science. You can start seeing increased profits by just following a systematic approach and having a clear strategy to work more efficiently and grow your customer base. The steps in this book are your roadmap; use them to set goals and keep yourself on the right course. One of the biggest risks on eBay is getting stuck in the realm of casual sellers and only doing things that are necessary here and now instead of coming up with ways to reduce or even eliminate a lot of these tasks.

The most profitable eBay sellers have learned how to do more in less time, get more people to see their listings, and get more buyers to come back again as repeat customers. Putting the advice in this book to work will not only directly help you do this but also open your mind to other ways you can get better and sell more. Some of the most effective eBay practices are discovered by solving individual problems as they present themselves, and when you're armed with a strategic mindset you'll constantly be thinking of ways to improve.

Chapter 7 – Inside the Power Seller Mind

So you've made it this far, and chances are you're already making some money on eBay. Pretty cool, isn't it? Told you there wasn't anything to it but to just get started doing it!

But you're not going to stop there. You want to learn how the big sellers on eBay do it, right? How to make more money. How to finally break free of those financial worries that keep you up at night and that nag you every single time you buy something you want but don't really need. Like that coffee this morning, or that lunch at the sandwich shop up the street from work.

Oh, the guilt. If only you had a little extra each month so you could just breathe easier. You're not looking for extravagance; you're looking for not having to poach from your savings all the time to cover you until payday. Or maybe having a savings to begin with.

Well, you're in the right place. This is where we're really going to get into the thought process that separates top eBay sellers from everyone else that's making $50 a month, or maybe every other month or just a few bucks here and there throughout the year.

But, we need to get one thing straight first.

The rest of this book isn't about step by step instructions or "blueprints" to follow. I already covered that in the beginning of this book and in my other book about eBay; so if you just skimmed them and didn't really take the time to thoroughly understand everything I definitely would recommend that you go back and do so right now, otherwise you won't benefit nearly as much from what you read here.

The rest of this book is about mindset, strategy, and how to become a smarter eBay seller so that instead of just making a little pocket change you can make money that will have a significant impact on your life. What qualifies as a significant impact? An amount that makes you able to do something that you previously weren't or that gets rid of a problem that you currently have.

There's no one-size-fits-all number that anyone can slap on it. Whatever it is for you, it's going to be different from the next person – but what you'll all have in common is that it'll in some way change your life for the better.

Ask around and you'll find that nearly everyone and their brother has tried to sell something on eBay at least once, but pretty much nobody has had any success with it and will look at you like you have two heads when you tell them you're poking around on eBay to make some extra cash because, they're absolutely certain, "that eBay stuff doesn't work…."

…which translates into "I tried to sell an old pair of jeans once and they didn't get any bids in a one-week auction so I gave up and said forget it all." And that's entirely true, if all you're doing is poking around. But if you poke regularly, and smartly, it's a much different story.

Remember, you're not trying to create the equivalent of a big chain department store here, you're trying to make a few thousand bucks to pay for your kids' preschool or travel soccer or to get out of debt or finally take that vacation you've been dreaming of for years.

The point is, when you're selling on eBay it doesn't have to be perfect. In fact, most of the time it doesn't even have to be all that good. I sold nearly $10,000 in my first six months of buckling down on eBay, and didn't even really know what I was doing for most of it. For the longest time I was selling junk from my house, I didn't even source products until I was almost half a year in.

Even today there are still tons of things I don't know and plenty of people who are more knowledgeable about eBay "under the hood" than I am. But I'm successful because I show up regularly. I've gotten into a consistent habit of finding stuff to sell, listing it, and repeating the cycle. Simple formula for success; just do the thing. So, if you're looking for something that gives you an A to Z list of what to do to get up and running on eBay, go back to the beginning of this book and read, then re-read if you didn't grasp all of it.

Now, if you're ready to learn how the best sellers and top money makers think creatively and work intelligently to make MORE money, then you're ready for the rest of this book. Within those few simple steps there are a ton of fine details that are the difference between a few bucks here and there and consistent, solid profits that can positively impact your quality of life.

But, a word of warning – if you're not already consistent about getting and listing things regularly none of the advice in this section will do you a lick of good.

OK, fairly warned. If you're ready, it's time to step inside…the mind of an eBay Power Seller!

Chapter 8 – Your Money Plan

You're probably wondering what those two things have to do with each other or better yet with you making money on eBay, right? Well have no fear, I promise that by the end of this chapter you'll see exactly how both give you great advice and motivation to sell successfully on eBay.

I've sold used swimming trunks on eBay. Many times. The first pair that I listed I honestly didn't expect to sell but they went in a matter of hours. (Note: eBay policy on selling used swimwear is that it has to be washed.) I put them in with like colors and strong detergent to get them all fresh and clean and ready for someone to hand me 15 bucks for, listed them, and the rest was history.

The next time I went thrift store hunting for stuff to sell I brought home another pair that sold in a few days. That's right, I paid my electric bill for the month in three days by selling stuff that two people's bare hides were in direct contact with. This is an extremely significant point to make because when you realize that it was profitable, and EASY, you'll start to see a whole new world of entrepreneurial possibilities open up.

It boggled my mind but just further proved the point that whatever it is, someone is looking for it on eBay. Might as well let them buy it from me instead if someone else.

My initial skepticism aside, I've since realized that the used swimwear category has some of the best margins around. A pair of trunks that cost $1.30 in the bargain bin at Goodwill or 50 cents at someone's garage sale can regularly fetch $15. Brilliant!

As for the hockey ticket, there's a big new market brought about by technology that I found out about entirely at random. A few years back my brother's girlfriend wanted to make him a collage of stuff from this San Jose Sharks hockey game they went to. The Sharks are his favorite team and they traveled a long way to see the game, since they live in Pennsylvania. Her only problem was that since the tickets were the kind that get emailed to you so you can print them at home, she didn't have an actual arena ticket stub to include in it to make it look all nice and memorable, just the printout with some loudmouth ad for a local pizza shop taking up half of the page.

Enter eBay.

A few minutes of searching and $10 later she had her "real" ticket stub and some guy had some cash for a so called piece of trash paper. The game wasn't anything historic like the first time this happened or a record for that or some player's 500th goal or any of that jazz, just a regular event that someone needed his ticket stub from.

Think about ALL of the sporting events and concerts out there that have switched to e-tickets for people who buy online and all of the season ticket holders or people who bought from the box office that have these 'souvenirs' left in their pocket afterward. Now you may not go scouring arena floors after you go to a game scarfing up ticket stubs (or you may, it's up to you), but that's not the point.

The point is, ALL kinds of so-called junk sells on eBay. Everything is worth money. Maybe not to you, but to someone else. I've sold old used baseball batting gloves on eBay. Seriously, these things were grimy and dirty and nothing that I wanted to ever touch my person again. But I took photos of them, showed all of these, uh, character marks, and described them clearly and accurately. And some dude bought them.

Just more of the tons of examples of things that you would never think can make money on eBay but do.

Your homework, as if this didn't get your head spinning, is simple – spend just ten minutes thinking of all the stuff you wouldn't immediately think of as profitable to sell that you have easy access to. Now look it up on eBay. Report back to me how much your mind is blown at what people will pay for. Better yet, skip the reporting step. Just go take some pictures and list it, and make yourself some money!

It's an opportunity just waiting for someone to go out there and take it. That someone might as well be you.

.

Chapter 9 – Not All Sales Are For Profit

"Wooooah," you're saying, "now hold on just a minute! I'm in this to make money, what the heck are you talking about?"

Relax – there's a totally legit explanation, and it's one that you're going to absolutely want to pay attention to and understand.

I'll repeat myself – not all sales are for profit. It's how this whole selling stuff thing works.

Ever wonder how in their right minds stores will mark prices down crazy low from time to time? Or why grocery store pharmacies offer free prescriptions? Or why cell phone carriers will just about give you a new phone for free when you sign up with them?

It's a lesson that anyone who is selling anything, regardless of what or where, needs to learn early on. If you focus on customer acquisition first, profit will follow in droves.

Let me explain. If you just list a bunch of stuff on eBay at the price you need to sell it for to make the profit you want, you'll make some money no doubt. But you'll be getting what I like to call "drop in sales" meaning people are just searching eBay and randomly find your item, it just so happens to be what they want and at a price they're willing to pay, so they buy it.

Great, you made a few bucks – that's never a bad thing. But the buyer has no clue who you are, likely won't remember you, and the next time that same person needs a similar item they're probably going to go right back through the search process instead of coming straight to you.

This is why your first objective should be to build your name, your brand, your recognition on eBay as this gives you a customer base. Think of how much easier it is to sell to someone who already knows you and has had a positive experience with you. They don't shop around, they come right back to you and make their next purchase. It doesn't take an MBA to figure out that your sales following this model will be much higher than just throwing items up and taking your chances.

So, how do you go about building this immensely valuable brand recognition? A few ways.

The first, and easiest, and also most overlooked, is simple old-fashioned customer interaction. When someone buys something from you, use the eBay message platform to send them a thank you note. Seriously. I know, it seems really odd, because so few sellers do it. When was the last time you bought something on eBay and got a message from the seller just thanking you for your purchase? In today's world of "communicate only when I have to and usually to deliver bad news or dispute something" doing this is incredibly refreshing and will leave an impression on your buyer.

Make sure to include your seller handle or store name in the message, so for example, a short line to the effect of *"Hi there – thanks for your purchase. Your item is shipping out today! Please come back to daves_deal_shack any time to check out our collection of model airplanes, there's sure to be more you'll like!"*

That's 34 words total, and you can even save it and just copy and paste each time. In other words, takes about zero effort and will set you apart from nearly all of the other sellers out there who are nameless, faceless account names on eBay. Remember, people buy things from people they like, so a little pleasantness will go a long way. Also, from a functional standpoint, sending a message like this leaves your name in the buyer's email and eBay message inbox – so even if they still don't remember your name the next time they're ready to buy they'll likely at least remember to go back through their messages to find the seller that was so nice to them and go right to you.

Another way to do this that's even more powerful is to send out a newsletter, if you have an eBay store. Now opening a store (a monthly subscription for a fee where you get more listings and some other additional marketing tools) isn't necessary to make a healthy profit on eBay but can be a viable option when you do the math on how much you're currently spending on fees. If you do go this route, one of those additional tools is the ability to create newsletters that buyers can subscribe to.

When you do this, you basically have a direct line to your customers – they'll get your newsletter and see what you have new for sale and can go buy from you, again bypassing the random search process. Making a strong call to action, as the term used in marketing is called, in your item descriptions and on your eBay Me page telling buyers to sign up for your newsletter to get notified about more great deals is how to get this ball rolling. Once you start getting newsletter subscribers you can build rapport with them so again, the next time they need to buy they're thinking of you as a known and trusted source instead of just another eBay seller.

These examples illustrate why your first priority should absolutely be acquiring customers and building a large base of people who know and are pleased with you. Once you have this, your sales will naturally increase because you have an audience to sell to instead of relying only on random drop-in buyers. Thus the idea that your early sales shouldn't be for profit. If you break even on an item because you priced it lower than you normally would to sell it quicker that's fine, because in the process you gained a customer (as long as you put to use either or both of the tactics here to 'capture' them for the future.)

It's in gaining customers that you make the real money, so focus on break-even sales early on and watch your customer base, and profits, grow and grow down the road.

Chapter 10 – Using Psychology to Sell More

Do you get frustrated when you have a bunch of watchers on your eBay items and then they end with nobody buying them? You just don't get it—if so many people are interested enough to watch then surely one of them should buy, right?

Seems to make sense, but that's not the case.

It's not until you start actually thinking about how people's minds work and what makes someone say 'Yes' to forking over their money that you're able to avoid this common pitfall and start making sales instead of just getting window shoppers.

In the majority of cases where a person looks at an item and marks it as a watch instead of buying it on the spot it's something that they like and want, but there's just a small detail keeping them from hitting the Buy It Now button right then and there. That something is more often than not, you guessed it, price.

Buyers will tell themselves they shouldn't buy something because they don't need it and can't really justify spending money on it, but want to leave the door open even though they know it's more than they want to spend. Watching an item gives them that secure feeling that they're not totally shutting down the possibility, so they'll mark it as a watch item and give the seller a false hope that there's a sale right around the corner.

Think about it, how many times have you done this in life, not just on eBay? Kept things for years instead of throwing them away even though they've been sitting in your closet for years untouched? (Gotcha – if you're reading this book you know by now you should be selling those things, not throwing them away!) Told a girl or a guy that you'll go out with them sometime even though you have no interest in them and just want to avoid awkwardly turning them down? Ate something that you know isn't healthy but justified it in some crazy obscure bending-of-the-facts-to-suit-your-desires way? Don't lie, we've all done it. Human psychology is amazing to study, but if you're going to even scratch the surface of it you might as well use it to your advantage and sell more now that you know how your buyers' minds are working.

eBay added the Best Offer feature so buyers and sellers can work through these small barriers and get to a price that will be agreeable for both. But it's more than that; it's an antidote to the no-hope-for-action window shopper that lets you make a sale instead. I started using it on all of my Buy it Now listings about a year ago and saw my sales go up immediately since I'm getting more buyers involved. The key is buyer engagement—getting the person on the other end that's mulling over your listing to actively be involved in the process; once you have them making moves it's far more likely that they're going to end up buying than if they just look and like but move on.

Using Best Offer just requires that you're prepared to do a bit of negotiating. When you have a buyer making an offer it's clear that they want the item, you just have to do the little dance that's necessary to find the sweet spot that works for both of you. You can set the Best Offer feature to automatically reject offers below a certain price, so you can weed out extreme lowballers who you don't even want to waste your time doing business with right from the start. You can also set it to automatically accept offers above a certain price, so if the buyer makes an offer that will definitely make you happy you don't have to do anything, it works just like a Buy it Now sale. That significantly cuts down on the amount of haggling you actually have to do.

For the remaining one-third of offers where you do get involved in some back and forth, just remember a few key points. Most notable, the buyer wants your item. If they're taking the time and making the effort to submit an offer, they're here to reach a deal. Work with them. Make a sale. Don't give your item away for next to no profit obviously, but selling at 80% of what you had hoped to get, especially if the listing has been up for a while, is better than not selling and netting 0% of what you had hoped for. It also shows the buyer that you're a decent person to do business with, and will likely open you up to repeat business form them if they're looking at an item you specialize in or they buy frequently.

The Best Offer feature allows both sides to make three rounds of offers, but honestly I've rarely had any go that far. Two exchanges is usually the max, since it goes like this. Let's assume a $40 item:

Buyer: "I'll offer $20 for this"

Me: "Can't go that low but will go do $35"

Buyer: "Offer $30"

Me: "Sold"

If I wanted to I could have split hairs and gone through one more round of this little do-si-do, but honestly, take the same if it's close to what you hope to get. Now of course if you're selling higher priced items it gets a little more serious since there's more money to be left on the table, but most of us are selling junk from our attic or the local Goodwill, so just get paid and move on to the next sale.

Takeaway here, people watch an item, especially a Buy it Now, because they don't want to give up the unrealistic idea of buying it. The truth is that they probably won't though, unless you give them a reason to get back in. That reason is Best Offer. It puts them in control again (or so they think) but what it's really doing is re-igniting that fire they have to get your used vase or shorts or CD collection or whatever.

Best Offer – use it!

Chapter 11 – Everyone Loves a Deal

One of my go-to tools in my sales boosting arsenal has been Markdown Manager. It has consistently generated increased activity for me and is something you can start using today to bump up your sales also. Markdown Manager is simply eBay's version of putting on a sale. The psychology of getting a deal is powerful to buyers and will drive them toward your listings.

Markdown Manager is another option only available if you have an eBay store, similar to the newsletter option that we discussed earlier. I'll stress again that having a store isn't imperative to making big money on eBay but once you get to a certain point it just makes sense because you pay less in listing and final value fees, aside from getting the other tools that come with it. So, if you do decide to make the leap to a store, you'll also want to start strategically marking things down to generate more visibility and interest in your items.

First, how to use it. Markdown Manager is very simple. On the 'My eBay' dashboard screen you just select 'Marketing Tools' from the list on the left hand side. Once on the Marketing Tools page you'll find Marketing Manager on the left side also.

From there you just follow the prompts to create your sale. You enter the start and end dates (note that you have the option to choose the time of day that your sale starts and ends also- these are in Pacific time so if you really want your sale to open up at a certain time make sure you convert the time zones) and whether you want to offer a fixed dollar amount off of each item or a percentage off. You can also choose if your sale should include all of your listings or only certain ones that you pick. If you list new items after your sale has started they won't have the sale discount applied to them automatically so you'll have to use the Edit feature on your sale to update it so they're included.

Knowing when and how to strategically use Markdown Manager to boost your sales is a little trickier. Far too often sellers get so eager just to make sales that they'll misuse this tool and slash their prices so low that they bring their profit down to almost nothing. To prevent this make sure you factor the discount into your starting price. Buyers will see through an item that's priced 20% higher but 'on sale' for 20% off, but you can make a small upward adjustment in your price if you plan to put an item on sale.

Basically the same as if you offer free shipping, you simply make your base price high enough so that the discount still gives the buyer a deal but doesn't totally strip you of profit. Remember, the goal is that your profit per item will be less but you'll make more sales overall.

The other consideration is that you don't want to always be running sales, as buyers will see through this too. Think of the furniture store you know that seems to always be going out of business, or the department store that always finds a reason to run a sale – most people realize these are just promotional gimmicks where the starting price is marked up.

Instead, try timing your sales to coincide with holidays or big shopping times such as back to school. If you run a weekend sale start it on Thursday to capture early birds and extend it all the way through Monday night to take advantage of the high viewing traffic that occurs then.

Finally, get as many people to know about your sale as possible. Include details on your next big discount on your newsletter to get your already satisfied customers to return to you - a sale is great for attracting 'drive by' business but is also a powerful tool to help you continue building your base of repeat customers.

So, the lesson here, if you go the store route – definitely make use of the Markdown Manager feature to take advantage of every buyer's love for a deal.

Chapter 12 – Making Sales that Others Don't

In this chapter I'm going to share with you some perfect examples of a small thing that can pay off exponentially in increased sales yet so many eBay sellers don't take the time to do, even though it's so simple and easy. It's going the extra mile to answer buyer questions and provide customer service, and it's almost like a lost are on eBay anymore. Always remember that you're dealing with real people at the other end of messages and transactions and if you treat people well and show them that you're knowledgeable and helpful you'll stand out to them over others who they're dealing with.

The first situation was a buyer asking about what other items I had after seeing one of my listings. Maybe it was too confusing for them to navigate; maybe they were just too lazy to read through it, who knows. The key takeaway is that I answered their question instead of just blowing them off or giving them some kind of canned response, and it turned into success for me. Here's their original message to me and my response:

Buyer: "Would you have anything in XXL Men's, like two shirts, prefer solids? Would you take $12 ea. and combine two in same shipping package? I will pay for these today…color is key. Thanks."

Me: "Hi there, are you only looking for short sleeve button down? In those I have a beige solid and a cream/off white with green and brown check pattern, both Polo Ralph Lauren size XXL. If you're looking *for other styles I also have Nike short sleeve polo shirt in orange solid size XXL. Yes, will do $12 each if you buy more than one."*

SO MANY sellers would just tell the buyer to 'look at my listings to see everything I have' in this case, but I went the extra step and did a search of my inventory and let them know exactly what I had in the way of what they were asking for. This took all of 2 minutes for me to do, but you'll see the results. I also made them feel like I was really there to help them out, so I asked what style and size they were looking for so I could be even more detailed. A little extra is what put me ahead of any other sellers this potential buyer asked the same question to; remember if a buyer wants to spend their money I'd rather it be with me than someone else, so I'll treat them right and be extra accommodating to them since 99% of other sellers will just see them as another question coming in.

After I let the person know what I had, they got back to me and not surprisingly said they were ready to buy. Here's where my 2 minutes earlier was well spent and absolutely worth the extra effort. This person also followed up with a message asking me to let them know whenever I got more similar items in stock!

Buyer: "My son only wants Ralph Lauren polo. He likes the polo shirts and the pocket t shirts. He does like the Guy Harvey t shirts also. He only wears XXL. Keep me on your list if you ever have these items."

Having a customer want to buy from you this way is definitely the 'next level' of customer service and something that most people selling on eBay don't put in the effort to do. When you think about how much easier it is to sell to a person who you've already demonstrated your knowledge and service to instead of someone randomly looking it's crazy why more sellers don't spend the time on this!

My other example comes from a person I negotiated a price with on a Best Offer listing. Same deal, instead of just treating them like a number I took the time to walk them through the process. Here is the key point where it all happened, they asked me to change the price on a listing to what we had just agreed to—I could have done that but told them that someone else could swoop in and buy the item in the time from when I updated it until they could purchase it, so I saved them from that risk and said they just had to make an offer for the price and I'd accept it:

Buyer: "You fix it to $17 and I will buy immediately."

Me: "If I change it to $17 someone else could buy it. Just counter offer and I'll accept."

Buyer: "Thank you, you're the best. I gave a great feedback."

And sure enough, their feedback read:

"Great seller, great guy, I appreciate honesty and I trust him."

So the point of these scenarios is that when you get buyer questions you literally have things teed up to hit a home run and win their business. Granted, basic questions about things like size aren't going to land sales if what you have truly isn't what the buyer is looking for, but cases like these where you take the time to really help them are going to set you up for sales and more importantly, repeat customers.

Remember – buyers are the only reason any of us are able to sell and make money on eBay, so when you get opportunities to help them out do it, you'll be glad you did!

Chapter 13 – What **NOT** to Do to Increase Sales

When I was first trying to grow my eBay store and make my operation more efficient (read: list and sell more stuff by doing less work) I got this great idea of how I could put together a master Excel spreadsheet that would be all coded up to create all of my listings for me. I pictured just punching in the brand, color, and size of each item and the sheet would do the rest, filling in the Item Specifics and writing the description, and I just hit upload into Turbo Lister and made a hundred new items in a minute.

My idea was entirely true—and was what big time eBay sellers do. Only problem was that I wasn't at that level yet and didn't have the time or the knowledge to do it in an efficient way since I was still working on eBay in my spare time. I spent most of the next two months working on this magic sheet and fine tuning the formulas in Excel, testing it with the Turbo Lister software, etc. All the while I WASN'T doing what had been bringing me success thus far—listing items regularly.

My thinking was "well, I'm going to focus on making this new system so in the long run even though I'm selling less now it'll pay off with way more sales in less time." Possibly true, but a bit farfetched for someone spending about an hour or two a day on this stuff. The only sales I made during this time were just odds and ends I had still listed randomly—but in the months leading up to starting this project I was clipping along at about a nice $500 profit per month.

Anyway, in the end my system DID work, but it was so difficult to maintain (my little tidbit of helpful advice on Turbo Lister - it's a great tool and yes, it's the way 'real' e-commerce businesses operate, but definitely not for beginner or even intermediate sellers) that I ended up scrapping it and going back to my previous one. My old way of making listings took a little more time for each individual one but in the long run was much faster because it was, most importantly, SIMPLE to me. Now I'm not advocating against automation and using technology to your advantage, whether it's Turbo Lister or anything else. In actuality, at some point you'll grow your operation large enough that it'll become as close to a necessity as can be if you want to continue selling more and more.

I'm simply illustrating another "Power Seller Mindset" principle as I like to call them, simply saying you have to work within your own capability and ultimately focus on what works. In my case, had I just stayed the course with what had been working for me since it was the best way for me to work given my available time and knowledge I'd be about a grand richer now—so I'm sharing this with you to help you keep one very important principle in mind:

Don't let great be the enemy of good enough.

To get up and running and become successful as a part time eBayer you only need to find a good enough method of generating listings in a small time, say a few minutes per item. Don't worry about .csv files and software uploads and linking to hosted photos and all of that jazz, it's just overcomplicating things for where you probably are now. Get good at the basics, and then get better at them. Save the advanced stuff for later, you may find that you don't even need it.

Your homework is this -- learn or come up with your own method to generate listings quickly. For example, if you sell a certain brand of shirts, make a listing for one and use it as a template each time you list more by going to the 'Sell Similar' function and just changing out the photos, size, color, measurements, etc. Use it, and tweak it until it works like a smooth running machine (the barometer for this is if you can make a new listing in about 2 to 3 minutes)—then keep using it. Don't try to go any further, let good enough be good enough and go sell stuff with it.

Because in the end, trying to get too sophisticated usually leads to outthinking yourself, when all the while you could have been selling things and making money.

Final Thoughts

I hope you enjoyed this book and not only learned some things you can put to use but also got motivated to develop a Power Seller mindset! While learning the "tricks of the trade" is a big part of being successful on eBay, having the right attitude, being a creative, out-of-the-box thinker, and simply finding ways to succeed with the resources at your disposal are just as important. My goal was to not only teach you some of the "X's and O's" of advanced selling, but also to inspire you to achieve on eBay and knock it out of the park!

If you enjoyed this book, there is one final thing I'd ask of you. Please leave a review wherever you purchased it. Just like asking for feedback from an eBay buyer, book reviews are a huge help for authors as well as other potential readers. So please take a few minutes right now to go and leave a review.

Thank you, and good luck in your selling!

www.ingramcontent.com/pod-product-compliance
Lightning Source LLC
Chambersburg PA
CBHW071810170526
45167CB00003B/1252